WHEELCHAIR WALKS in Devon

Lucinda Ruth Gardner

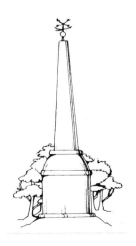

OBELISK PUBLICATIONS

GW01071963

Some Other Titles from Obelisk

Diary of a Dartmoor Walker, *Chips Barber*
Diary of a Devonshire Walker, *Chips Barber*
Ten Family Walks on Dartmoor, *Sally and Chips Barber*
Ten Family Walks in East Devon, *Sally and Chips Barber*
Walks in the South Hams, *Brian Carter*
Pub Walks in the South Hams, *Brian Carter*
Haunted Pubs in Devon, *Sally and Chips Barber*
Ghastly and Ghostly Devon, *Sally and Chips Barber*
Dark and Dastardly Dartmoor, *Sally and Chips Barber*
Weird and Wonderful Dartmoor, *Sally and Chips Barber*
(Films and TV Programmes) Made in Devon, *Chips Barber & David FitzGerald*
Beautiful Dartmoor, *Chips Barber*
Beautiful Exeter, *Chips Barber*
From The Dart to The Start, *Chips Barber*
Burgh Island and Bigbury Bay, *Chips Barber and Judy Chard*
Boat Trip Down the Dart, *Bob Mann*

For further details of these or any of our titles, please send an SAE to Obelisk Publications at the address below, or telephone (01392) 468556

Dedicated to my mum
whose love, courage and laughter showed me how to cope with adversity.

Acknowledgements

This is my chance to say thank you to Michael Denning for his help in making this book possible and for his opinion, advice and humour from the wheelchair. Also thanks to Barrie Anderson for his assistance with pushing, pulling and wonderful photographs.

Plate Acknowledgements

Sketch maps by Sally Barber
Photographs by Chips Barber on pages: 9–21,25,26,28,30 and 31
Photographs by Barrie Anderson on pages: 3–8,24,27,29 and 32

First published in 1995 by
Obelisk Publications, 2 Church Hill, Pinhoe, Exeter, Devon
Designed by Chips and Sally Barber
Typeset by Sally Barber
Printed in Great Britain by
The Devonshire Press Limited, Torquay, Devon

Wheelchair Walks

Wheelchair Walks in Devon

Foreword by Chips Barber

Books come to be written for many different reasons and this book is no exception – it is the happy outcome of a series of semi-related circumstances.

I have written various books, quite a few about walking, and these have led to talks to interested groups of people, many of whom are not able to cope with the demands of hill or coastal walking. So I'm often asked about easier strolls or ones that can be done with wheelchairs or prams. Having been challenged in this way I used my regular local radio spot to appeal to people in the area for suggestions of suitable walks of this type. One particularly helpful listener was Michael Denning, a former professional dancer, now in a wheelchair himself, who offered to try out any route that I thought might be suitable and let me know the 'pitfalls'. However, this was impractical, Michael living in Cornwall and me, many miles away, in Devon.

This was where Michael's carer, Lucinda Gardner, stepped in from out of the shadows and offered to write and research the book. After all, someone in her position was perfectly placed to relate the practical considerations involved in tackling such outings. About the same time we noticed in the press that BT were looking to sponsor efforts for helping the disabled to get out and enjoy the countryside, so thanks must be extended to them for helping an idea become a certainty.

And so we come, from village halls, over the air waves, down the telephone line, along some hard and dusty tracks, to the pages of this book, which will open up lots of opportunities for wheelchair walkers in Devon.

Lucinda's pleasant, easy-to-read descriptions will show you what a treat is in store when you do these walks. This, of course, is provided that you heed the advice or any warnings given! Take great care and enjoy yourself.

— 1 —
TIVERTON CANAL

Situated in mid-Devon under the auspices of Devon County Council is the Grand Western Canal Country Park. This follows the canal from Tiverton to Lowdwells, a distance of 11¼ miles in total, and can be found seven miles from the M5 when leaving at junction 27. On the approach to Tiverton follow the brown 'symbol' signposts for the Grand Western Canal, which will bring you into the car park, where at the far end you will find parking bays for the disabled designated by the wheelchair symbol painted on the tarmac. There is no charge for parking but donations are welcomed towards the upkeep of the country park.

Once in the wheelchair, before commencing your journey, you may like to visit the toilet (RADAR), which is situated near the entrance to the car park and from where, by climbing a short sharp zig-zag ramp you are at the Canal basin and the start of an enjoyable walk.

An Act was obtained in 1796 for the construction of the Grand Western Canal with the aim that the transport of goods could take place between Taunton, Tiverton and Bristol. Due to a combination of the Napoleonic Wars, rising costs and increased wages, work did not start until 1810. By 1814 the section from Tiverton to Lowdwells was completed. The transportation of lime was particularly relevant to Tiverton and the first lime kilns were built in 1829 where the lime was fed directly onto the barges. Evidence of the lime kilns can still be viewed today from the canal basin and the car park. Canal traffic declined as the railway took over and, when a serious leak occurred in 1924 resulting in the canal being divided in two, commercial traffic virtually ceased. The British Waterways Board in 1971 allowed the Devon County Council to make the Canal available for recreation, so allowing thousands of visitors to enjoy the serenity of the meandering waterway.

As the essence of any canal is that it is as level as possible this walk is ideal for wheelchair users and also a pleasure for any attendants propelling the wheelchair. The surface is smooth compacted earth with a light covering of sand and shingle and is of a good width.

From the panorama of the Canal Basin we decided that a walk to Milestone-III would make a comfortable three hour walk in which to enjoy the sunshine and scenery. Before setting off the teabar/restaurant (a converted barge moored on the canal) proved just too

tempting and, although a wheelchair cannot gain access into the barge because of steps, there are picnic tables situated on the grass where we tucked into tea and hand-baked cakes. Replete, the tow path and canal snaked in front of us, well populated with wild life including ducks, swans, fish and hiding moorhens among the water lilies. Shortly into the walk you can see the base of a former bridge, which still has grooves for a stop gate should the canal need to be shut off in an emergency. The next bridge you come to is the modern William Authers footbridge, constructed in spring 1991 to connect a school and housing estate. On both sides of the canal there are houses with their gardens reaching down to the water, but this scenery gently gives way to pasture and farming land. The second bridge to negotiate is Tidcombe, which is situated on a fairly sharp bend. Care is needed as you go underneath the bridge as the paving stones can become wet and muddy and there isn't a vast allowance of space either side of the wheels. In view on the right is a large house, which was once Tidcombe Rectory, today its function is that of a Marie Curie Nursing home. Here on the left is also the Milestone-I although the inscription is now illegible. Soon you come to a tall oak tree-lined section below which is the valley of the River Loman, this proceeds on to the Warnicombe Bridge. Again take care unless you are interested in wheelchair water sports!

The scenery has now changed to shady woodland and we spotted a squirrel making good use of the branches. From here approximately half a mile farther on is Manley Bridge (this has stone masons' marks on both parapets) and following the straight stretch of tow path you can see Milestone-II. With no effort, but much enjoyment, we had already completed two-thirds of the outward journey, enjoying the peace and tranquillity of the walk but still eager to find the 'delights' around the next corner.

The stop gate grooves can easily be seen on East Manley Bridge (also the turning place for the horse-drawn barge) and, after the canal has curved beside the road for a short distance, the aqueduct comes into view as the next marker. Built in 1847 the aqueduct is 40 feet above the former railway line and the name of Kerslake, Engineer, Exeter can be seen just above the waterline on the south side of the cast iron trough. A wharf was situated just beyond the aqueduct where road stone was unloaded. From now the path is not so well trodden but still remains very wheelchair friendly, though, as in most cases, the wetter months make the going more difficult.

Now comes the only bridge on this section of the walk that you cannot pass underneath. This is Crownhill or Change Path Bridge and carries a byroad to Lower Town, Halberton. You can cross the bridge via a slope and a wooden gate, over the small road and through another gate on the other side. The slope down this side is grassy and of a moderate gradient. Very shortly the Tiverton Road Bridge is reached (the most difficult to pass under on this walk), and beneath this sandstone bridge can clearly be seen some more stone masons' marks. The canal now takes a sharp bend and here we find Milestone-III.

On the opposite side of the canal and bridge is a car park and picnic area (the site of a wharf where stone was unloaded and crushed for use in road

making), which could be used if you wished this to be your starting point. But, the Tiverton Road Bridge carries a lot of fairly fast traffic and has no pavements. These factors combined with the fact that the bridge is fairly narrow means that great care needs to be taken if you wish to cross, especially if you are in a wheelchair.

As mentioned before, this walk is virtually completely level and invites the participants to walk as far as they feel able. There are seats and benches along the way and plenty to enjoy viewing, including the fishermen and the horse-drawn barge.

Back at the Canal Basin is a shop and booking office in a building that was originally a stone stable for the barge horses. On sale are a variety of gifts, souvenirs, ice-cream, permits for those wishing to fish and booking facilities for those planning to travel on the barge. The horse-drawn barge operates roughly from April to September but access is down three steps with a handrail either side.

Overall this walk made an extremely pleasant afternoon, the good surfaces, easy gradients and tranquil scenes making it a walk to recommend. Don't forget your camera, a few tasty morsels from your picnic for the ducks, and maybe even a shovel and bucket for the environmentally friendly way to treat the roses – courtesy of the horses!

— 2 —
BREATHTAKING BELLEVER

'Breathtaking Bellever' is a very apt description as this approximately two and a half mile walk is certainly the most taxing we completed and should only be attempted either with an electric wheelchair or if all members of the party are physically fit.

The setting for this walk is the area of Postbridge lying in the East Dart River valley. It is reached along the B3212 with car parks situated on either side of the road. For the purpose of this walk we chose the car park over the cattle grid at the Bellever turning, but, if you should decide that the walk is too steep or you would rather enjoy the views over a picnic, then park in the Information Centre car park which has designated disabled bays. There is also access to the picnic area and a disabled toilet (newly built and of a good standard). You would do well to avoid viewing the inside of the Centre during busy periods as the space is limited.

Having parked and locked the car (please do not leave valuables in the car especially on view), the wooden gate marks the entrance to your intrepid journey! Stretching ahead of you is 'The Lich Way', an ancient track, which led from the east side of Dartmoor to Lydford. The name 'Lich Way' means 'road of the dead' a literal meaning as until the thirteenth century everyone within the limits of the Forest of Dartmoor and within the Parish of Lydford had to take sacraments and bury the dead by going over the moor to Lydford church. When this practice ceased the path still remained in use as the Forest Courts were held at Lydford. Proceeding at the pace of a cortege, head straight up the hill. Alternatively, before the steep climb begins, there is a track to the right, this runs

parallel to the B3212, it is wide and level so you can enjoy the forest without the exertion. However, the track climbs at the other end and the only option is to retrace your wheel tracks. Following the Bellever Tor signposts, proceed along the wide track with its compact surface. Three quarters of the way up the climb is a seat which allows time for reflection over the panorama of the moor (in truth it provided me with a chance to enable my heart to settle back in my chest and my puce complexion to return to a ruddy glow!)

After this interlude continue the last quarter of the climb and follow the track as it curves to the right (still following the Bellever Tor signs). The wide logging track continues on a fairly level plane, on one side the forest is partially cleared and the logs are stacked high awaiting collection. At the cross roads of the tracks is a sign post. Turn left at this post following the yellow cycle track directions. You have now completed approximately one mile. The scenery is dense forest, which is part of the 1,000 acres of Bellever Forest bought from the Royal Duchy of Cornwall by the Forestry Commission in 1931. Included in the original planting, which took place in 1921, were Douglas Fir, larch, beech and Sitka Spruce. Today, depending on their quality, the trees are used for construction, pallets, fence stakes, chipwood and pulp. This part of the walk brings you as near to nature as it is possible to reach in a wheelchair.

Until now the surface has been very good but as you drop downwards it deteriorates. Take this part slowly for you will soon come upon a turning to the left (270°) which is where the cycle path will take you back on your return journey. Dropping away to the right is the valley and woodland with its tracks but, by keeping to the path as it gradually descends, you come to a small level clearing which allows a vista of the moor, heathland and a small holding.

One last burst of energy is needed for the final part of the insidious climb as the track finally links with the 'Lich Way' a few hundred feet beyond the seat. Past the 'Christmas trees' everything is now downhill! (It takes almost as much effort to stop the wheelchair running away as it does pushing uphill and a zig-zag transverse course may be the easiest and safest way down.)

Before you leave for home, visit the clapper bridge which spans the river a few yards downstream from the road bridge. A word of warning – although the kerbs have been lowered the pavement is very narrow and uneven. The alternative of pushing on the road is not suitable due to the speed of the traffic, narrowness of width and an obscured driver's view because of the road bridge. If, after careful negotiation, you manage to reach the clapper bridge, you will see a mediaeval construction, which spans 42 feet 8 inches and consists of nine stupendous slabs of granite. This was built on the site of an earlier ford and meant that travellers on their way to Tavistock and Chagford could cross the river even when it was in full spate.

'Breathless Bellever' is not a comfortable stroll on a Sunday afternoon but very few times with the wheelchair are we able to experience the sheer exhilaration that comes with viewing the beauty and raw power of the moor in situ without the limiting constraints the chair can sometimes bring. This experience can be yours at Bellever.

Wheelchair Walks

— 3 —
DALLYING IN DARTMOUTH

Within the South Hams, a designated area of outstanding natural beauty, situated at the mouth of the deep water estuary of the River Dart, lies the town of Dartmouth. Depending on your direction of approach, the town can be reached via the A379, A3122 (formerly B3207) or, for a more unusual trip across on one of the car ferries from Kingswear, A3022 and B3205.

Dartmouth is a town steeped in history. For over 900 years sailors have left in times of peace, on voyages of discovery, on missions of trade and, from the Crusades to the Spanish Armada, to enter into combat and do battle. Original settlers could be found inhabiting the steep sides of the valley around Townstal (referred to in the Doomsday Book, 1086) but the level waterfront area of Dartmouth is ideal to dawdle and dally in the wheelchair and see glimpses of the past whilst enjoying the present.

Entering this very popular holiday resort on the A3122 our route took us down Townstal Road, College Way, Coombe Road and turning right (A379) into the North Embankment. We were extremely lucky and managed to park on the roadside at the north end of the Embankment (parking is restricted to two hours for the summer season but vehicles displaying a valid orange badge can remain all day). However, as Dartmouth is extremely popular with the public and roadside parking is soon filled, an alternative is to use the Mayor's Avenue Car Park (246 places) which has allocated disabled parking bays. At present, as in any other South Hams Council car park, there is no charge for cars displaying a legitimate orange badge and clock. It is worth mentioning that the handicapped toilet is situated in Royal Avenue Gardens linked by a pathway to the Mayor's Avenue Car Park. This is a unisex toilet, fairly basic in facilities and does not operate a key system.

The History of Dartmouth is quite colourful – it rapidly developed over a period of 100 years when the French saw its potential as a sheltered haven opposite Normandy and the Channel Islands. In 1147, 164 ships set sail for the Second Crusade and part of the fleet left from Dartmouth to join Richard The Lionheart for the Third Crusade (1190). Evidence of the developing trade between Dartmouth and Bordeaux can be seen around the town today in the form of grapes carved on wooden buildings. This came about when Henry II married Eleanor of Aquitaine and British wool was swapped for French wine. The first mayor of Dartmouth came after Edward III granted a Royal Charter to the town if it would provide two ships of war when the King demanded. Two such ships were necessary when twelve ships sailed to join Drake fighting the Spanish Armada in 1588. Prosperity grew during the sixteenth to eighteenth centuries, goods were taken to the settlers in Newfoundland, cod and salt were then loaded and taken to the Mediterranean and exchanged for fruit and wine. Steamships became an important feature of the river with 700 ships visiting to refuel at its peak. In 1905 maritime pursuits were enhanced by the Dartmouth Royal College, which can still be seen today. Connections with France continued but this time the 485 ships leaving Dartmouth (mainly US force) left to attack the Normandy Beaches. Today trading ships have been replaced with a multitude of leisure crafts.

Starting the walk on the very flat 'herringbone' paved North Embankment, we ambled along looking across the River Dart to the views of Kingswear. One of the nicest sights is of the steam train chugging into the station with the visual puffs of steam and the audible 'toots'! The North Embankment merges into the South Embankment as you near the centre of town. There are plenty of seats along the promenade, which allow ample opportunity to stop and just enjoy the marine activities before you. Kiosks are situated on the very wide pavement, their function is to sell tickets for the various boat trips down the River Dart. With 13 miles of tidal water and a myriad of coastal scenes there is plenty to delight the optical senses. Sights include Britannia Royal Naval College, the shipyard

Bayards Cove

where Chay Blyth's yacht *British Steel* was built, and 'Greenway' the birthplace of Sir Humphrey Gilbert (latterly the home of Agatha Christie). Certain trips on board these boats are suitable for wheelchair travellers and any enquiries to the Companies elicit a considered and helpful response. At the end of the embankment is 'The Cannon', an 18-pounder cast iron gun, which was cast at Briansk in Russia in 1826. It is assumed that it was brought back from the Crimean War as a trophy.

Turning right into Cole's Court you quickly come to Lower Street where you have the option of turning left or right. To the left is the lower car ferry and beyond that 'Bayards Cove'. This is a fascinating historical part of Dartmouth but it is cobbled with a very narrow and difficult to negotiate pavement and therefore does not provide an ideal environment for a wheelchair. However, if you

decided to proceed (a slow pace is suggested if the look of the wheelchair occupant is anything to go by!) you will find yourself in the same area as the Pilgrim Fathers who set sail from here in 1620 in the *Mayflower* and the *Speedwell*. More recently the Cove was used to film scenes in the BBC series *The Onedin Line*. After this delightful diversion, or if the decision was to turn right, the next road to explore is Lower Street. There are a variety of small shops, some which are accessible some not, and exercise caution with the traffic and the pavements. Soon you will find yourself in the centre of the town, now turn left into Duke Street. Facing you on the right is the seventeenth century Butterwalk. This Merchants House was built for Mark Hawkins between 1635-1640 and today houses a museum and restaurant. After admiring the carved heads, grapes and mythical beasts, cross the road and then turn right into Foss Street, which is now pedestrianised. Here are a variety of interesting shops including an accessible coffee shop on the corner (Devon cream teas are available!). This is very different to the past when Foss Street was a dam to retain the Mill pool where its waters were harnessed to drive two mill wheels. The Mayor of Dartmouth in the fourteenth century (John Hauley) had warehouses on the east side where sailing ships could unload.

After exploring Foss Street the easiest route for the wheelchair is to turn right into Flavel Street, which can be found about two thirds of the way down Foss Street. This short passage will connect you to the Royal Avenue Gardens. Again eminently suitable for wheelchairs, there are plenty of areas to stop, admire the flower beds, and let the world go by.

As you can see there is plenty to experience in Dartmouth and, providing you stay at the lower levels, it is a pleasant and untaxing walk which we enhanced with an ice-cream in Royal Avenue Gardens and, overlooking the River Dart, freshly caught fish and chips eaten straight from the paper!

— 4 —
MOUNT EDGCUMBE COUNTRY PARK

Whether you have a couple of hours to spare or a whole day, few places can provide the scope for such entertainment as the 865 acres on the Rame Peninsular that form Mount Edgcumbe Country Park. This corner of Cornwall was legally a part of Devon until 1844, perhaps reason enough for inclusion in this book?

To reach the park from Cornwall follow the A38 to Trerulefoot roundabout, then the A374 and B3247 to Crafthole, Millbrook and Mount Edgcumbe. If your approach is from Plymouth the journey will take you via the Torpoint Ferry (a car carrying ferry) to Antony on the A374 then to Mount Edgcumbe on the B3247. There is a pedestrian ferry that travels from Admirals Hard (Devon) to Cremyll (Cornwall) but this is not suitable for wheelchairs.

Several options are available for parking, the most convenient is on the level beside the water's edge, literally at the end of the road leading to the park. However the area reserved for disabled parking is not very large so tends to get full quite early. Please don't be tempted to park behind the first row of cars as this area needs to be kept clear for emergency vehicles and is also a turning space for the buses serving the Cremyll Ferry. There is a car park provided a few yards up the road but here you will have to contend with a gravel surface. One further choice is to park next to Edgcumbe House (this is the car park that is well signposted with the blue and white wheelchair symbol) and is ideal for those wishing to view the house but, if like ourselves, you wish to walk through the park and gardens, it is at the top of quite a steep climb, which we suggest you only attempt if using an electric wheelchair or if the pusher regularly works out in the gym! There are about six 'green passes' which allow disabled drivers holding Orange Badges to park within the Park – these can be obtained from the Visitor Centre Shop and must be displayed prominently in the front of the car. The rules concerning eligibility and observance must be adhered to for safety reasons as the park rangers need to know exactly how many vehicles are in the park in case of an emergency.

The Park is a Grade One historic garden and forms part of the South East Cornwall Heritage Coast with scenery ranging from formal gardens to rugged coastline. In 1971 the park was purchased from the Estate of the 6th Earl of Mount Edgcumbe by Cornwall County Council and Plymouth City Council with the help of the Countryside Commission. It is the only country park in Cornwall.

Entering the park you will find on the left the aforementioned Visitors Centre providing leaflets, information and an array of gifts. Following the path to the left and then under the arch (situated here during the winter months is the Camellia Tea Room open daily from 11.00–3.30) you will pass over a small patch of cobblestones and then come upon the first of the formal gardens. This is the Italian Garden with the impressive

Doric style Orangery. One quick aside, positioned behind the Orangery are toilet facilities including a handicapped convenience. There is no need for a key, ample space inside, and, even if the Orangery Restaurant is closed the toilets remain open. Today you are able to obtain a good range of food and drinks in the Orangery Restaurant, which is open daily from April 1st until October 31st. In previous times the orange trees were grown in large tubs, which had wheels for ease of movement, these were kept in the Orangery during the winter months then took their places lining the gravel paths. The centre piece is a marble fountain (a present to Richard, 2nd Earl, from Lord Bessborough) and, at the southern end is a balustrade, mounted on top of which are the three figures of Bacchus, Venus of Medica and Apollo of the Belvedere. The bust of Aristo lies in a niche under the centre statue. Pushing or wheeling around this garden is very easy and a beautiful place to while away as many minutes or hours as you please. Separating the formal gardens are the very fine examples of Ilex Oak which form hedges of some 20 feet in height.

Leaving this garden by the footpath alongside the coast you will start a slight climb. The path can be a little uneven and sometimes muddy but it is perfectly negotiable. At the top of the sloping lawn to the right is a Thomson seat which must provide a view of the sailing activities on the Plymouth Sound. Soon will appear the old blockhouse, the oldest building in the park. This was constructed during the reign of Henry VIII as a defence of the river mouth, its partner can be found on the opposite side of the estuary. A more recent building in front of the blockhouse is a saluting battery, which was remounted in 1880 with twenty-one eight pounders taken from a French frigate, the firing of the guns now being used to welcome visitors. Taking the path that runs beside the blockhouse will lead you into the second formal garden.

The French Garden displays regular shaped flower beds, which are enclosed by twelve inch high box hedging with a shell fountain and fish pond in the centre. Here is the Conservatory, a south-facing single-storey building, and an urn dedicated to the memory of Sophia, Countess Mount Edgcumbe. Negotiating these narrow but flat paths, follow

the laurel hedges to the left and you will enter the open lawns of the English Garden.

This garden is less formal and actually contains many examples of foreign and tropical vegetation, including palms, Lebanese cedars, bamboos, Magnolias and cork trees. A sheltered spot, you may want to dally here for a while taking in the splendour of the Garden House, a Doric temple which was enlarged at the end of the eighteenth century by the addition of two rooms at the side, a study and a boudoir. Continue wandering the pathways past the Garden House and you will discover the newly created American and

New Zealand gardens. Look out for the geyser, which sprays high at regular intervals. It would be difficult to describe these paths to follow by route, and we suggest that you just explore those that take your fancy and find suitable for the wheelchair. Presuming that you have found your way back to the English Garden take the widest, gravelled path which will bring you out through the high Bay Tree hedge and on the coast path walk. Before leaving the garden you can find the Grotto, this is a pet's cemetery found only recently when the Joint Authority gardeners were clearing the undergrowth. Features of the Grotto include a lion's head which spouts water.

Back on the path, proceed carefully on the last piece of bumpy ground before you reach the smoother paths leading from Barn Pool. This is an ideal spot for having a picnic on the open grassland with the waters lapping the beach. Follow the signpost for the 'House, Upper Park and Cremyll Ferry' and start to climb on the return part of this circular walk. Arriving shortly at a 'T' junction you have two choices, downwards to the entrance gates and your car, or, upwards to the house. Be warned, the climb to the house is very taxing and, if you would like to visit the house and Earl's Gardens, then taking the car is a much easier option. Travelling the last part of this walk as you effortlessly wheel down the tree-lined avenue means there is plenty of opportunity to digest the magnificent vistas before you. At the bottom, turn around and look upwards to the splendour of the house. This has been the Mount Edgcumbe residence from 1553-1987. The house was gutted by incendiary bombs on April 22nd, 1941, and rebuilt to the original sixteenth century design by the 6th Earl of Mount Edgcumbe and the architect Adrian Gilbert Scott. The house is now open to the public on a limited basis and, according to a park ranger we spoke to, has a lift inside to accommodate wheelchairs.

Although we have given you a suggested route, the seven acres of formal gardens and 800 acres land of mean there is plenty for you to explore and enjoy in your own way and time.

— 5 —
SHIPLEY BRIDGE AND THE AVON DAM RESERVOIR

One of the most beautiful locations on Dartmoor that is suitable for wheelchair users is Shipley Bridge. To reach this destination we took the turning signposted 'Avon Dam' at the Marley Head junction on the A38. The roads from here wend their narrow tracks across Dartmoor and require careful negotiation especially in the summer months when the world and his wife are desirous of visiting the area. There is a small car park at Shipley Bridge, which has two disabled spaces at its far end next to the toilets. If you happen to choose a particularly popular day, parking could be a problem as a sloping grass verge is not always to be recommended for the disembarking of a wheelchair!

Assuming that you have parked the car, there is a disabled toilet available (no key is required) which can prove useful as the walk is beside running water! Unfortunately these toilets are only open during the season and South Brent would be the nearest village.

With a picnic packed, prepare to tackle the northerly walk of approximately one and a half miles each way. The surface for this walk is probably the best of the walks attempted in this book, its quality is of road standard thanks to the joint care of South West Water and Dartmoor National Park Authority. Although the climb to the bottom reaches of Avon Dam is of a gentle gradient, it is rather insidious and does have an aerobic quality if attempted in one go.

Immediately enjoying the running waters of the River Avon on your right hand side as it tumbles over the granite rocks and boulders, you will soon see on the left hand side a large rock which is the Hunters' Stone. On closer examination

The Hunters' Stone

you will be able to see the names engraved of local huntsmen who rode Dartmoor. Pressing on upwards, the flat grass verges by the picturesque river make an ideal stopping place if you need to catch your breath or just to enjoy the vista. It was a lovely sunny day when we explored, and to add to our delight was the sight

of four small children, shoes and socks neatly placed on a large boulder, splashing and frolicking in the cool Avon water.

Two large stone pillars stand guard either side of a wooden gate. This gate was locked but there is a way around to the left hand side. In times past this gateway was the entrance to Brentmoor House (demolished in the late 1960s), and the profusion of rhododendrons that would once have graced the grounds are still in evidence. If you look carefully as you round the corner you can see the memorial stone dedicated to a little girl who died here.

You now have a chance to cross the River Avon, without getting your wheels and feet wet, as a road bridge now follows the east bank as it climbs relentlessly northwards. Within a very short distance from the start of your journey the scenery has changed and the beauty of the rough moorland now becomes apparent. A big bonus, the only time we encountered this on any of our walks, was the appearance of the moorland ponies and moorland cattle. Very used to the passage of two-legged visitors they gave the wheelchair no more than a cursory glance before continuing with the all-consuming job of feeding.

Once more the road takes you across the river, this time a look to your right will show the impressive structure namely Avon Dam. In the wheelchair it is possible to reach the flat grassy verges at the bottom of the dam beside the pumping station. With your eyes cast heavenward the splendour of this construction is apparent and, if your imagination will allow, picture the 305 million gallons of water that the 50-acre reservoir can hold. The dam and reservoir took three years to construct, finally being completed in 1957. With a catchment area of 3125 acres and the notorious Dartmoor rainfall it is not hard to see how it provides water for the South Hams and Torbay areas.

When the time comes to retrace the wheel tracks homewards, it is a lovely amble back to the car park allowing your full attention to be focused on the scenery and not on the effort of propelling. Depending on the time of year chosen there could well be an ice cream van at the bottom, little can be nicer than enjoying an ice cream by the clean sparkling waters of the Avon.

— 6 —
STROLLING AROUND STOVER COUNTRY PARK

Stover Country Park can be found approximately 14 miles from Exeter and 33 miles from Plymouth, very close to the junction of the A38 and A382, near Newton Abbot. From the junction on the A38 head towards Newton Abbot on the A382 and after 100 yards you will find the entrance to Stover Country Park on your left. You will see that there are numerous parking zones spread among the trees. Designated handicapped parking spaces can be found if you go beyond the Information Centre and turn right. You may find it useful to pick up a leaflet describing the park from the Information Centre (this is up a couple of steps).

The Park, now managed by Devon County Council, provides a circular walk of approximately one and a half miles around a lake so rich in wild life it has been declared a Site of Special Scientific Interest. If you allow a minimum of one hour for this walk on the smooth compacted earth that forms the path, the delights of the Park will be revealed to you. One word of warning, although there are portable toilets to be found in the car park, they are not particularly suitable for the disabled and certainly not suitable for wheelchair users. A well-known super store is located nearby, which may provide better facilities.

From the handicapped parking zone a path leads gently down to the lakeside walk. There are other access points, but this one seems easiest. As the lakeside route is circular, it doesn't matter very much which direction you start your journey. Try to memorise the appearance of your starting point otherwise you might miss it and start going round again! If you have time this would be no hardship as the walk presents no difficulties to either wheelchair occupant or pusher.

The 14-acre lake and its surrounding woodland is teeming with birds and wildlife. You might wish to bring some scraps for the ducks, swans, squirrels and others but they are well provided for by the feeders hanging among the trees and, the continuation of the 110

species is encouraged by providing over 100 bird boxes in a wide range of designs. The lake earned its Site of Special Scientific Interest status in 1984 for its importance to dragonflies. The woodland is particularly lovely in the Spring when the Rhododendrons are in flower.

At the far side of the lake you will find a potential diversion from the circular walk. At a bridge over a narrow creek you will see that paths head off along both banks of the creek. The paths go for approximately 500 yards to a spot known as the Cascades. Here they meet via a footbridge thus forming a loop around the creek. According to the Devon

County Council leaflet this route is described as suitable for wheelchairs (the yellow marking on the map) but our experience on the day suggests that this is not quite so. There are two steps on the side of the footpath and four on the other. Furthermore, the paths are narrow and bumpy with tree roots protruding, which can make the trip

a little perilous, this is in contrast with the lakeside path which is smooth and danger free. However, if you feel tempted to explore this area (and why not?) then we would suggest that you take the path on the right – as you stand with your back to the lake – and be prepared to return by the same path.

As you travel around the lake there are plenty of opportunities to see the wildlife including the cheeky squirrels, beautiful butterflies, basking adders, lizards and different varieties of ducks on the lake. Placed around the water's edge you will find display boards describing and identifying the land and water inhabitants. These boards have been thoughtfully placed at a height so they can be read by those in wheelchairs.

You may wish to spend half a day or even longer in the Country Park and the picnic areas in the woodland are provided equipped with tables and benches. There may also be an ice-cream van near the Information Centre. This Park could probably be very popular on Summer weekends and during the peak holiday periods. Bear this in mind if you wish to fully appreciate the beauty of Stover Country Park.

— 7 —
TOURING TAVISTOCK

On the banks of the River Tavy is Tavistock. Originally a Saxon camp it developed when a Benedictine Abbey was founded in AD 974. Today it is the largest town in West Devon and can be found via the A390, A384 or A386.

We arrived in Tavistock on a sunny Tuesday morning and found the town full of hustle and bustle. Parking in the allocated spaces in the Bedford car park, opposite the bus station in Canal Road (there is no charge at present for vehicles displaying a valid orange badge), we set off to explore the area.

A short level walk quickly took us into Bedford Square where there is a comprehensive Tourist Information Centre. Unfortunately there is one very high step into the shop, manageable with a strong pusher behind, but, the staff will assist by bringing the information to you for those who are unable or reluctant to attempt the step.

Tavistock has a good range of wheelchair accessible shops and the Pannier Market (first held in 1105) is well worth exploring. This traditional charter Pannier Market takes place every Friday, Tuesdays boasts a craft and antique market and on Wednesdays is the Victorian market.

After lunch in the town we set off for our walk, first checking the Guildhall toilet which operates a RADAR key system, then down the tarmaced path alongside the River Tavy. From here we crossed the park by the bandstand and walked beside the canal, well populated with ducks and ducklings ready for any picnic offerings! This is very easy pushing and a comfortable ride in the wheelchair but became slightly less agreeable as we went down the narrow grass track to the gate at the bottom of the park, the only accessible exit for a wheelchair, but, if bumping on this track does not appeal to you, this can be avoided by following the River Tavy through the park. Crossing the main road (automated pedestrian crossing) we started the Drake's Walk. Access commences through a gate especially for wheelchairs and the walk has been developed with the wheelchair user in mind. The ground is level and takes the width of the chair though a little care is needed passing cyclists and pedestrians. Unfortunately many dogs are exercised along this route so caution is needed with regard to the placement of one's wheels! With the Tavistock Community College on one side and allotments plus a newly constructed housing estate on the other, you may be forgiven for thinking that although the walk is wheelchair-friendly it is hardly visually stunning. Have patience, shortly you will arrive at an attractive mixed woodland. This provides the chance to observe woodland wildlife and on our chosen day the trees provided a pleasant shade from the glaring sun. The canal

was the achievement of an engineer called John Taylor (1779-1863) and connects the Rivers Tavy and Tamar at the old river port of Morwellham. Possibly some of the first iron barges used on English canals were seen here transporting their cargoes of tin, copper, lead, iron and silver. Today the canal provides leisure facilities for canoeists. After approximately one mile (1¹/₂ km) you will come to a group of farm buildings on the left hand side known as Crowndale Farm, site of the alleged birthplace of Sir Francis Drake. If you have enjoyed this walk and feel it is of an acceptable level of effort for the propellant and of comfort for the wheelchair occupant **turn back now**! If, however, you would like to persevere and follow the canal from Crowndale Stone Bridge to Shillamill viaduct for no other reason than it exists, then carry on. New requirements will be a sense of determination, a sense of humour, plenty of cushions and a wheelchair safety belt!

The track from here on is mud which, although firm for most of its length, proved to be very boggy in patches even after a particularly dry summer period (tip: dragging a chair backwards through these patches is easier and hopefully keeps the chair occupant in situ rather than on their nose in the mud). Tranquillity and peace added to the sheer feeling of being able to achieve what other walkers take for granted are the great benefits of this walk. For those doing the pushing it can be quite an exertion through some of the boggy patches but it is a very level walk, for those in the chair it can be slightly harrowing as the path is narrow and falls away steeply to one side with the dark waters of the canal to the other (this is a place to consider staying friends with those pushing you!) Eventually you will see Shillamill viaduct (originally used to carry the trains between Tavistock and Bere Alston). We managed to get the chair through a swinging gate but great care is needed due to deep pits and jutting stones, then through the gap in a fallen tree that has had a section cut out to allow access for walkers. This is fairly narrow but allowed our chair through at an approximate overall width of 22 inches. Finally we reached the end of the path for the wheelchair and stopped for refreshments before retracing our steps and wheelchair tracks the four miles (approximately) back to Tavistock.

This walk provides the opportunity to do as much or as little as you feel able on the day. Stroll around the town and dally with the ducks in the park or chat with the canoeists on the canal and relive the routes of the iron barges as you pass through the gentle woodland. If you felt able to tackle the full walk then hopefully you will also feel satisfaction from your adventure in the country.

— 8 —
TEIGNMOUTH

On the South Devon coast, located at the mouth of the River Teign is the holiday town of Teignmouth. Providing the ideal venue for a flat seaside walk, it may be reached by either the A379 or A381. If you take our suggested promenade it covers approximately two miles in either direction on a level, good surface.

Way back in time Teignmouth was not one town but two separate and distinct settlements. These were united in the mid thirteenth century when the Crown granted them markets. Its past history includes being producers of salt (the Doomsday Book mentions 24 salt works), a fishing centre, shipbuilding yards and a thriving port. The New Quay was built in 1821, its primary function to transport the granite which came from Dartmoor and was used to build part of London Bridge. From here also was shipped the ball clay mined in the Bovey Basin. This trade continues today, the ball clay being used for earthenware, tiles, insulators, paints and some rubber products.

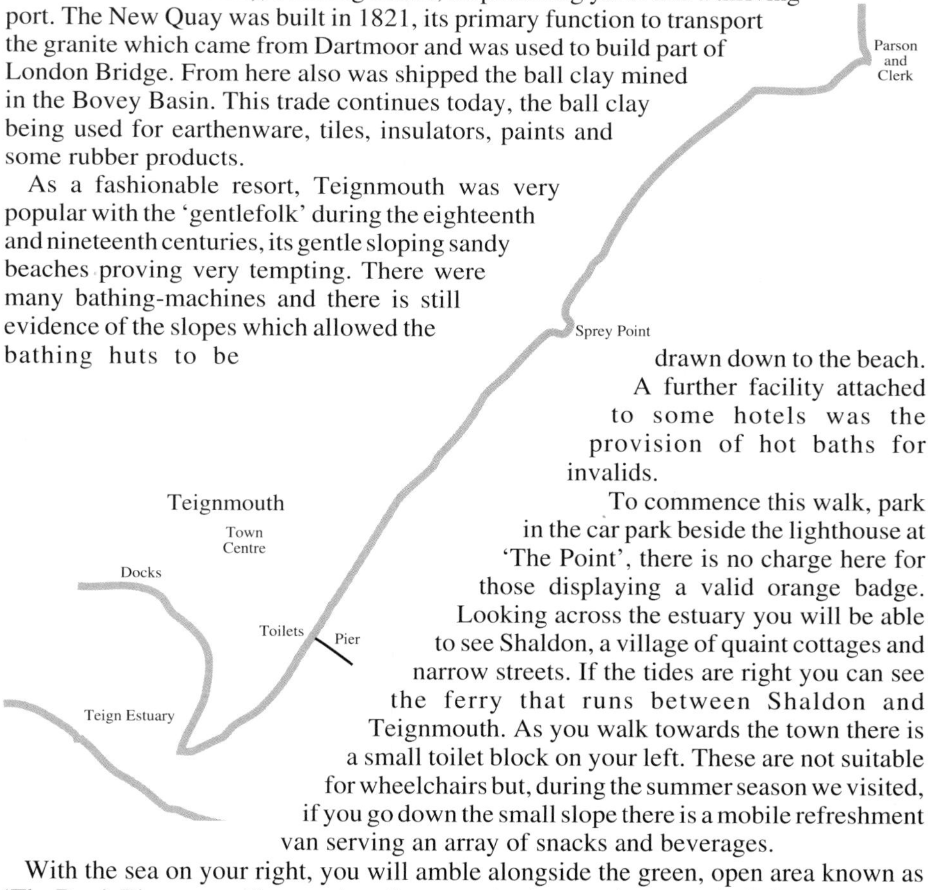

As a fashionable resort, Teignmouth was very popular with the 'gentlefolk' during the eighteenth and nineteenth centuries, its gentle sloping sandy beaches proving very tempting. There were many bathing-machines and there is still evidence of the slopes which allowed the bathing huts to be

Parson and Clerk

Sprey Point

Teignmouth Town Centre

Docks

Toilets Pier

Teign Estuary

drawn down to the beach. A further facility attached to some hotels was the provision of hot baths for invalids.

To commence this walk, park in the car park beside the lighthouse at 'The Point', there is no charge here for those displaying a valid orange badge. Looking across the estuary you will be able to see Shaldon, a village of quaint cottages and narrow streets. If the tides are right you can see the ferry that runs between Shaldon and Teignmouth. As you walk towards the town there is a small toilet block on your left. These are not suitable for wheelchairs but, during the summer season we visited, if you go down the small slope there is a mobile refreshment van serving an array of snacks and beverages.

With the sea on your right, you will amble alongside the green, open area known as 'The Den'. There are still examples of some early nineteenth century buildings to be seen here. If you should need one there is a handicapped toilet situated here, once more an example of the RADAR scheme. This park includes a children's paddling pool, bowling green and tennis courts. For those who fancy the diversion, there is Teignmouth pier, today full of electronic games.

Continue past the pier, enjoying the sea bathers as they splash in the inviting waters. The walk will merge into Courtenay Place, Den Promenade and Terrace Walk. There has been recent work done here and the slopes are wheelchair friendly. The walk now having left the town area, runs beside the railway with East Cliff forming an impressive

backdrop. One element of amusement is the sign prohibiting wheeled vehicles beyond this point – we carried on! With a pebble type of surface it is still a reasonable ride in the chair and very comfortable pushing. Should you wish to stay with friends or family on the beach itself, there are two slopes down to the sand.

Past Sprey Point you will be on the Sea Wall Promenade. With a sheer drop down to the beach it is prudent to stay close to the wall beside the rail track. The surface also has patches where it is uneven so **please take care**. In view now is the outcrop of rock known as 'The Parson and the Clerk' and this walk terminates when the rail track enters the tunnel. There are steps that lead under the track but these obviously are not suitable for wheelchairs (there are toilets here for any attendants that may need them).

Turning back to return to Teignmouth will give you the chance to view the area from a different perspective. There is peace to be enjoyed here (until a train thunders very near by on this still well-used railway track – it helps to have good nerves!), but as you near the resort it is enlivening to be caught in the holiday atmosphere. There is always the reward of a Devon ice-cream as you sit and watch the tide come in.

The Parson and Clerk

— 9 —
TARKA TRAIL BIDEFORD TO INSTOW

The full Tarka Trail stretches for a distance of 180 miles, a footpath following the route described in the classic novel by Henry Williamson *Tarka the Otter*. Part of this trail is also a cycle path using the path of a disused railway line, which, being level, is ideal for our type of journey.

Situated on the banks of the River Torridge, the town of Bideford (which can be translated as Little White town) in the county of North Devon is our starting point. The A39(T) or the A388 will bring you to the town. Crossing the old Bideford Bridge, you may notice that the arches are of different sizes. The reason for this lies in the past when the amount donated by the individual traders corresponded with the size of their businesses. Another interesting fact is that this bridge is said to rest on rafts of wool. Follow the brown sign posts for the trail by turning right at the small roundabout, down a narrow street. Keep following this street which soon runs into a track beside the industrial developments and builders yards. Be careful as there are some quite deep potholes in places. Although you will probably feel that you have somehow missed your turning, persevere and a signpost denoting the parking area will come into view. This is a 'free for all' car park but it provides a level and easy access to the cycle path.

The time to allow for this walk is about two and a half to three hours return and it is

probably now appropriate to mention that there are no handicapped toilet facilities at either this end of the walk, or, at our destination of Instow. However, there are toilets in Bideford town in Victoria Park, which lies beside the River Torridge. If you have the time, the lower reaches of Bideford town are very interesting to explore and you can wander the river bank on this side by using the newly completed Landiviesau Walk (certain areas around the trees are cobbled and need a little careful negotiation should you decide to go this way).

Back to our walk. With the river on your left hand side you are in the valley of the River Torridge, an area regarded today as one of great landscape value. Our journey starts as we enter 'East-the-Water' and come upon the old signal box which has been restored and now houses a small collection of photographs and railway memorabilia. Further into the station there is still in place a section of railway track and residing on it is a 1950s converted railway carriage. This also serves refreshments, is an information centre and houses exhibitions. Unfortunately the few steps mean it is not wheelchair accessible. The building on the right is the old Bideford 'East-the-Water' station, completed in 1872, and, has since acted as a branch of the 'Midland' bank and also a restaurant. When the railway was functional it ran from Barnstaple to Meeth, its main job to transport clay from the Marland and Meeth works to Bideford. Coal was mined in 'East-the-Water' until 1960 and a disused tunnel passes beneath the railway, once upon a time the route for coal to the quayside. One piece of trivia is that the extracted pigment from the coal known as 'Bideford Black' was used in paints and cosmetics (there is still a cosmetics factory 'East-the-Water' today but the ingredients are unlikely to be the same!)

If you decide to pause here and look over Bideford town then you may like to consider the history of the building that can be viewed just across the bridge on your left. This is the Royal Hotel. Once a colonial building it also served time as a gaol. Past famous residents during its time as a hotel include the clergyman and author 'Charles Kingsley' famous for his novel *Westward Ho!*.

Pushing on with your travels you will notice that the surface is very smooth and compacted, so, combined with the virtually flat terrain the only consideration is how far you actually wish to proceed. Bideford stretches upwards on your left, its various buildings mingling together in the hillside. Along the quayside the boats bob on the water or nestle on the bottom depending on the flux of the tide. In front of you the new Bideford Bridge can be seen, a tall impressive structure but very much a contrast when compared with the beauty of the original bridge that can still be seen if you look over your shoulder. Below the new bridge now stands a small new housing estate but this ground once housed the Bideford ship yard.

The setting allows the wheelchair user excellent visibility of the estuary as you aim towards Instow. By looking to the right a large house can be seen near the skyline in a woodland setting. This is Tapley House and Park, open to the public and owned by the Christie family. It is said that this house is one of the most haunted in South West England.

On the opposite bank is the imposing structure that forms the Appledore shipyard. This has housed, through the years, some of the largest and smallest vessels, its presence making a large contribution to the local economy. As your vision becomes restricted due to the trees and greenery on both sides of the path, there is evidence of past industries, namely a lime kiln which has been exposed for viewing.

Still strolling along at a comfortable pace you will soon reach Instow Yacht club. This is actually housed on the remainder of the station. There is still one platform in evidence, which, if you feel like attempting the slope, is a lovely vantage point to stop and enjoy the view. The signal box that you can see was built in 1861 and is the only one of its kind remaining in South West England. It has the status of a Grade II listed building.

With the crossing gates ahead you have now reached the town of Instow. This is a lovely 'turn around place' for your walk and very worthy of further exploration. Turn left after going through the swing gate next to the crossing gates. Either pavement is suitable for the wheelchair. Instow was a small hamlet until the nineteenth century when the passion for seaside bathing and holidays led to its development. The railways helped with this growth by bringing holiday makers to the area (it also transported clay from Fremington quay to 'inland'). The sands at Instow are flat and golden and due to a raised platform area on the pavement there is a very good vision vantage point for wheelchairs. Appledore is just one of the things to be spied, the pretty fishing town with its very narrow streets lies directly opposite, (once said to include the second homes of several *Coronation Street* stars). Refreshments are available by either visiting the ice-cream van, holiday shops and cafes, or, in grand style at the impressive hotel whose lawns slope downwards to the road.

If you should feel like extending your walk then go through the swing gate the other side of the crossing. Here the verdant banks are steep either side of the pathway and soon you will come to the railway tunnel. This is paved and there is 24-hour lighting but watch out for the odd drip (the water variety!) As you wheel onwards the scenery changes to sand dunes and an array of wooden homes now line the path. On one side these give way to a marine camp from where you can sometimes see the amphibious vehicles travel down and enter the water. It is at this road crossing that for today we finished our walk. After a quick look at the Instow Cricket Club house, especially attractive with its thatched roof, we took a saunter to the estuary to see the views across to Braunton Burrows.

Although the railway line was once a heavily industrialised area it is now a haven for a variety of wildlife. You can spot lizards, butterflies and various species of river birds including shelduck, oystercatchers, gulls and lapwings. For those not in wheelchairs there is Isley Marsh, an RSPB reserve, especially important for waders and wildfowl. This can be found by Yelland Power Station farther along the trail. Although you will not be able to cross into the reserve via the stile in your chair, the marshy estuary lands run beside the path allowing a certain amount of viewing.

To recap, this walk is extremely wheelchair-friendly and certainly not taxing for those pushing. There is a good variety of scenery and the choice of stopping and starting at many different points. However, one word of warning, this is also a cycle path and an extremely popular one at that. During the summer months a convoy of 60-plus children passed us, and, although they were extremely well behaved there is the occasional cyclist who travels by at an excessive speed. An appeal now to those riding bikes – please fit your cycles with bells, which would allow those travelling at a slower pace notice of their impending presence. Follow the beautiful 'Tarka Trail' and take time to enjoy the countryside that was so vividly described in *Tarka the Otter*.

A circular walk of approximately one mile on a purpose-made path in Forestry Commission land. This comparatively short walk would make an ideal 'taster' for the rest of the walks in this book. It is undemanding but delightful.

Mamhead Forest is not the easiest place to find. Travelling by car from the Exeter direction, follow the A38 westbound to the A380 fork. After about half a mile on the A380, take the first exit left – near the top of Telegraph Hill – signposted "Mamhead". Follow this road for approximately one mile until reaching a fork – take the right-hand road. You will shortly come to a crossroad (where you must halt and give way to traffic from left and right). Carry on straight across this junction for half a mile and you will see the entrance to Mamhead Forest Walks on the left.

Please note that if you are travelling from the Plymouth direction, it is possible to reach this location by leaving the A38 at the Devon and Exeter Race Course. Take care with the subsequent crossing of the highspeed A380.

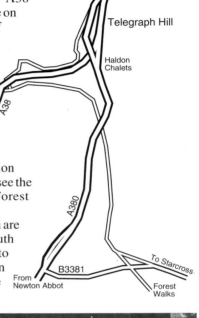

There is plenty of level parking available at Mamhead but you will find it helpful if you park as near as you can to the information board. On studying the board you will see that three walks are indicated by different coloured dots on a map. The yellow route is described as an "all-ability walk" and this is the one recommended here. The walks are apparently meant to be signed by way-posts bearing appropriately-coloured roundels. Indeed, this seems to be the case with the red and blue routes. However we found no trace of yellow marks when we visited – have they faded? Were they ever there? Are we particularly unobservant?

As it happens, the answers to these questions are not really relevant as identifying the "yellow" route is quite easy. All the walks share the same path at the outset and, at the divergence, the yellow route is distinguished by its wide, smooth surface. You may be interested to note that cyclists are banned from these paths.

The walk is, as you might expect, mainly bordered by trees on both sides. The shade and the forest fragrances enhance the tranquillity of this beautiful spot. Be prepared, however, for one stunning view over the River Exe and Exmouth. Also look out for the extraordinary obelisk, the history of which you can learn from the information board.

It is possible to tootle round this walk fairly quickly, but there is no need to rush – this is very much a place to linger. There are plenty of benches located along the walk and these could make fine picnic spots. We did start to explore one of the other routes but were soon confronted by a fallen tree. Furthermore, the path was bumpy and hard-going in places. For the best of Mamhead Forest stick to the "yellow" path.

There are no toilet facilities of any kind here but as the walk can be easily completed in an hour it hopefully will not present a problem. Nearby the large city of Exeter has several disabled toilets.

There has been a deliberate effort made here to make provision for those in wheelchairs and the result is very satisfactory. It is a pleasure to share with our friends as they perambulate, the sights, sounds and fragrances of the Devon countryside.

— 11 —
THE HAVEN TO DOUBLE LOCKS, EXETER

If you would like to spend around five hours exploring the banks of the River Exe and the Exeter Ship Canal then may we suggest this walk. It has the added bonus of visiting a lively canal-side pub as the destination!

The start of this walk is at The Haven, Exeter, which is on the periphery of the City centre. This is in the vicinity of The Quay and The Canal Basin, both of which have been developed into residential and recreational areas in recent years. Arriving by car, turn

into Haven Road off Alphington Road (A377) near central Exeter. Follow the brown signs for the Maritime Museum. Park in Haven Banks Car Park, which is run by Exeter City Council and provides parking spaces for the disabled.

Leave the Car Park by the footpath at the north corner and head towards the Maritime Museum. From here you can choose to continue along Haven Road or go around the Canal Basin – either way, you aim to cross the River Exe using Cricklepit Bridge (a suspension footbridge). Once across the blue bridge, turn right and head towards The Quay. This has become a popular area of Exeter and has lots of facilities, including toilets for the disabled. From here travel more-or-less south along the east hank of the River Exe. After passing a weir, the path does a short dogleg (to avoid a bijou development) and then you turn right to cross the river by another suspension footbridge.

On the other side of this bridge, the path does a quick right and left and you come to a cycle-track along which you proceed left. Please note that although this is a designated cycle-track it is not exclusively for cyclists. All the paths so far have been tarmaced and of an excellent quality for wheelchair travel. The track eventually curves right to bring you to Clapperbrook Swingbridge where a road crosses the Ship Canal. Do not cross the swingbridge but turn left along the road. It may be best to use the gravel surface to the right-hand side of the road, as the popularity of the public house at its end is reflected in the amount of traffic. You will soon come to Double Locks, the most interesting feature of which is, arguably, the eponymous Hotel rather than the pair of lock gates. I must confess it felt like we approached the inn at what seemed like 40 mph – this was either due to the slight gradient before the pub entrance or thirst!

It is worth mentioning that the Double Locks Hotel is open all day (except Sundays when it's 12–3 p.m. and 7–10.30 p.m.). Food is served all day, but be warned – at busy times you may have to wait up to 30 minutes for your order to arrive. I can assure you that it is worth waiting for. While you are waiting, you might find it worthwhile to inspect the ceiling of the Public Bar. Note, too, that the Hotel has a toilet for the disabled.

After visiting the Double Locks Hotel you may return along the same route by which you arrived. Alternatively, the more adventurous may indulge in some variations. For example, you could cross the lock gates and return to Clapperbrook Swingbridge on the opposite bank of the Canal. A wheelchair rider needs the assistance of two strongish persons due to the high steps at either end of the gates – but it's perfectly safe otherwise. If you chose to cross the lock gates it is possible to remain on this side of the Canal beyond the Swingbridge, indeed, this is a more direct route back to the Car Park – but it does skirt some industrial zones and may not appeal.

Another variation would be to continue straight on along the cycle-track instead of turning right via the footbridge to The Quay. This would give you the choice of returning to The Canal Basin or directly to the Car Park.

Whichever path you decide to take there is plenty to experience as you wander by the water. You will have passed the majestic swans on the River Exe, chuckled at the antics of the ducks as they splash in the weir, enjoyed the sights of the canoeists on the canal, and savoured the food and liquid refreshment at the 'Double Locks'!